FAITH-BASED LEADERSHIP AND MANAGEMENT

how personal viewpoints & values
influence an organization

THEODORE H. KITTELL

GlobalEdAdvance
Press

Faith-based Leadership and Management
How Personal Viewpoints and Values Influence an Organization

Copyright © 2011 by Theodore H. Kittell

Library of Congress Control Number: 2011941797

ISBN 978-1-935434-07-8

Kittell, Theodore H., 1934 -

Subject Codes and Description: 1. BUS071000: Business and Economics: Leadership; 2. REL028000: Religion: Ethics; 3. BUS041000: Business and Economics: Management - General

All rights reserved, including the right to reproduce this book or any part thereof in any form, except for inclusion of brief quotations in a review, without the written permission of the author and GlobalEdAdvancePRESS.

Cover design by Barton Green

Printed in the United States of America

The Press does not have ownership of the contents of a book; this is the author's work and the author owns the copyright. All theory, concepts, constructs, and perspectives are those of the author and not necessarily the Press. They are presented for open and free discussion of the issues involved. All comments and feedback should be directed to the Email: [comments4author@aol.com] and the comments will be forwarded to the author for response.

GlobalEd Advance Press
www.gea-books.com

DEDICATED TO MY WIFE,

Martha,

WHO ASSISTED ME WITH THIS BOOK.

~

Paulette Carrier was a great help proofreading the manuscript.

My appreciation is also expressed to those who read my book "Christianity and Management," which focused on Servant Leadership, and asked for more information on how to become a successful Business Leader.

Contents

Introduction 9

Exploring the Differences 14

Working with People 22

Practical Work Applications 32

Selecting the People 44

Troubleshooting 50

Supervising 58

Business Law 70

Administrative Potpourri 78

Managerial Communications 98

Epilogue 106

Appendix One: Ancient Writings 111

Appendix Two: Useful Books 113

About the Author 117

The Power of Thought will assist one to undertake things that seem impossible. This power of thought is the secret of all inspiration and all genius. Becoming inspired is to get off the beaten path and out of the rut, because extraordinary results need extraordinary means. When one comes to recognition that the source of all power comes from within, the source of inspiration is tapped.

--Paraphrased from *"The Master Key System,"* Charles F. Hannel (1912) and published in 1916.

Introduction

Personal viewpoints and values are major factors that impact the daily struggle of leaders and managers. This is true in all aspects of life, but especially true at the place of work. Most organized enterprises today talk about good business to guide the required effort to achieve a profitable status. However, saying the right words is the easy part; doing the work to make the words happen is the struggle. This is where faith-based principles and values influence the decision and behavior process in organizations.

A sequel to "Christianity and Management" (2003), this book focuses on Leaders and Managers. Leader refers to the top level office or CEO of an organization. The next level of officers; such as, Department Head down to the level of those who supervise other people, is identified as managerial.

Various topics are presented to differentiate between leader and manager, as well as the qualities found in successful leaders regardless of title or level of operation. Some concepts from my previous book are presented to establish a foundation for those who have not been in my classes or read my previous volume.

Business operates in a complex world of change. How does your business create stability in the unstable times? The best way to remain stable is to stay true to basic beliefs and values. This requires a moral and ethical commitment by everyone involved in the business. Each employee has a part to play from the custodian to the CEO.

Faith-based Operations

Many organizational leaders find conflict with the secular styles of leadership/management and their personal beliefs and values. There are many similarities between secular management and faith-based operations, but there are also profound differences, this is true particularly in regard to working with and dealing with people.

Do faith-based leaders and managers hold themselves to a higher level of ethics than a purely secular operation? A purely secular organization normally has the "profit motive" as a core principle of the operation. In contrast, a faith-based operation should function controlled by a "people motive" that relates to the well-being and satisfaction of both customers and employees. Bottom-line profit is a natural outcome of a satisfied customer base and a positive work force in an efficiently run business.

There is further contract between the secular and the faith-based leadership/management. The secular defines management as getting work done through or at the expense of others. This gives secular managers an opportunity to control and exploit the work force. On the other hand, a faith-based mind-set understanding guides leaders and managers in meeting the needs of people as they work to accomplish operational goals. Using this approach the employees have a mind to work and the leadership/management team has more satisfaction in the performance of their duties.

Another important aspect of a faith-based approach is to adequately train people to be equipped to do their job well. When workers feel adequate for the assigned tasks, their satisfaction and production levels are elevated. When workers feel they are served by the organization, they are more apt to view their work in a more positive way. The sky is the limit when there is fairness and equity in the workplace. When workers feel thankful for having a pleasant place to earn a living for their family, production usually is on the increase.

Most organizational problems fall into three basic categories. (1) Basic commitment to clearly defined goals. (2) Lack of unity among workers and between departments, and (3) poor communication. In most cases, poor communication causes the other two problems. By learning the skill of identifying the basic cause of a problem usually enables those in charge to lead in solving the problem.

Approximately five decades ago there was a split in the approach to management training from an academic perspective. One group approached the teaching of management with the perception that managers were rational technicians who applied the principles of management science in the work place. The other group taught from the management perspective that managers were craftsmen who practice an art that could not be acquired through scientific principles.

It would be useful for faith-based groups to become familiar with the two approaches to management theory. How one works with others can be improved when they know the way another manager approaches the work and the people. The servant leadership approach to management is for the most part the best approach to management.

Faith-based Principles Make a Difference

Starting with the Ten Commandments from the Torah and appearing in various forms in other religions to the Golden Rule in the New Testament, we are stewards of both the instructions and the resources God provides. The Golden Rule is so basic it appears in most of the religions of the world. For example:

- **Buddhism** – "Hurt not others in ways that you yourself would find hurtful" (Udana-Vaarga 5,1)
- **Christianity** – "As you would that men should do unto you, do you also to them likewise." (Luke 6:31)
- **Hinduism** – "This is the sum of duty; do naught unto others what you would not have them do unto you." (Mahabharata 5, 1517)
- **Judaism** – "What is hateful to you, do not do to your fellowman. This is the entire Law; all the rest is commentary." (Talmud, Shabbat 3id)
- **Taoism** – "Regard your neighbor's gain as your gain, and your neighbor's loss as your own loss." (Tai Shang Kan Yin P'ien)

II

EXPLORING THE DIFFERENCES

There are definitely differences between being a manager and being a leader. These clear differences should be examined and understood to adequately function in either role or position.

A Manager is basically **extrinsic** - coming from without the person. Behavior does not come inherently from within the person. A manager is guided by organizational rules and does not function on the basis of personal values. The manager is primarily concerned with the well-being of the whole organization or operation. This could be called shepherd management because of the concern for the whole and not necessarily the parts. A manager serves the company.

A Leader is **intrinsic** - coming from within a person. Behavior is based on the real nature of a person's beliefs and values. The basic and essential feature of a leader demonstrates real concern for the people involved, both the customer base and the work force. This concern for people is built-in to the fabric of the inner core of the person. This quality is essential to influence people to follow the leader toward stated goals. This could be called servant leadership.

Manager is **behavioral** - a person's behavior, conduct or actions is based on the rules of the organization and the existing condition or circumstance. A manager responds based on a specific set of conditions in a manner determined by the rules of the organization.

Leader is **psychological** – a leader's treatment of others comes from personal values deep within the psyche. Leaders are moved by the needs of others. They are touched by the desires of others. Leaders are disturbed by the same conditions that make others unhappy. A leader is open and expressive and clearly demonstrates a sensitive nature. A real leader normally has an inspiring personality and is appreciated by those who follow.

A Manager operates within a framework of formal or positional authority based on the guidelines of the organization. This authority identifies the manager as an officer bound by prescribed and established rules. A manager has little personal discretion, this makes a true manager almost totally objective, this provides the ability to perceive and describe a circumstance without being influenced by personal emotions or prejudices. Once an objective decision is made a manager behaves in an organized and precise manner.

A Leader operates based on personal influence without the use of positional authority. Provided the leader in question is the CEO, the authority rests in the leader, but a true leader functions in the informal realm using personal influence. This influence is the power that affects a person or circumstance in a positive direction. The ability to influence others is the power to affect the thinking and behavior of other people. This together with the force of a positive personality creates the force of servant leadership.

Exploring the Differences

A manager is controlled by the rules and culture of the organization. Although a leader is generally governed by the organizational culture, as a leader more personal decisions are made within the broad confines of the organizational climate. At time the leader must step outside the norm and do what is right for the individuals involved; this should to be done without doing harm to the organization.

A manager is closely controlled by the principles governing conduct as specified by the company is normally unwilling to take risks. A risk opens the door for something to go wrong and good managers avoid such possibilities. Leaders on the other hand, understand that without risk taking there would be no positive business results. All organizations must manage risk to remain stable and profitable, yet to be in business is itself a risk taking venture. There no guarantees that a particular product will sell or that a individual employee will be productive, or that a "brand" will maintain a leadership position over time. This is where leaders and managers, in spite of their different perspectives, must work together for the good of both the organization and the people.

Leaders focus on people. A Manager concentrates on what is best for the organization and deals with the bits and pieces of organizational progress. Leaders establish simple goals that anyone can understand; managers promote the *status quo* of the organization.

These points will provide some insight into the differences between a manager and a leader.

Depending on the size of your business you can be a leader of if your business is small you can function in both roles. Call this what you may: a one-man show, a leader/manager, or a manager/leader. When one person leads an organization, this person must become all things to all in order to move things forward. In such case, it is vital that you remember to change hats now and then to adequately function and move the things forward. You must always know which hat you are wearing or you could behave in the wrong way at the wrong time, in the wrong place, to the wrong people. It is better to be right! Always know which hat is on your head.

Quality

Quality is important to every business whether you are a manager or a leader. If you want the general standard of a product or service, you must clearly understand the meaning of quality. Some ideas about quality include:

1. **Confidence** that the quality in your work output is uniform and meets or exceeds the general standard or grade expected. The product of service must of the highest or finest standard and delivered in a timely manner. This provides confidence in both production and personnel. A good motto: "Promise less; deliver more."
2. **Fitness** or suitability of the product or service for the intended use. Does your

product or service meet the advertised criteria? If not you do not have the quality you need to sell your product. Fitness does not mean you are meeting the design standards. Fitness is determined by whether the product is selling or the service is useful in the marketplace.

3. **Reliability** or dependability of the product or service. Were the customers satisfied? Were users satisfied over an extended period? the product performing its intended function for a length of time? Time specified in the warranty is a standard for the minimum length of time. The customer usually expects longer use of the product than the warranty.

Exercising Leadership

- Leaders assist others in progress toward personal achievements and goals. When the people achieve the leader succeeds.

- Leaders must always model the high standards that are expected to govern personnel: "Good enough" is not good enough! Only the best product or service will succeed in today's world.

- Leaders should always see room for improvement.

- Leaders follow a plan; the people follow the leader. This is the proper way to implement a plan.

- Leaders must have and live by a grounded set of values.
- Leaders must do what is right.
- Leaders give credit where credit is due.
- Leaders who demonstrate loyalty to associates will receive allegiance in return.
- Leaders use sensible judgment in guiding others.
- Leaders influence best by example.
- Leaders encourage teamwork and reward the team.
- Leaders have frequent contact with the people in the organization and seek feedback.
- Leaders progress and deal with needs as they arise.
- Leaders use coaching as a means of influence.
- Leaders understand that there are organizational goals and individual goals and behaves based on this knowledge.
- Leaders use coaching as a means of correction and guidance.

*A Manager
concentrates on the
organization.*

*

*A Leader
focuses on the people.*

FAITH-BASED LEADERSHIP & MANAGEMENT

III

WORKING WITH PEOPLE

Working with people involves many different and difficult aspects on human interaction. The approach of leadership to people within a given organization depends on whether the person sees themselves as a manager or as a leader. A manager in the course of being administrative must make decisions as to work performance issues and conformance of workers with rules and regulations of the organization. A leader on the other hand relates in a more positive manner with workers in the performance of responsible leadership and regular duties. Of course, the size of a business organization determines how involved leadership and managers are with people.

The leaders contact with most workers will be through the managers who are in daily contact with the work force. The exception may be the leader who leads by walking around the enterprise without regard to the size of the operation. A leader that leads this way has to be careful that this behavior does not undermine the manager who relates daily with personnel.

Desirable or Essential Qualities

Organizations search for personnel they believe to be both pleasing and advantageous to the product or service delivered by the business. These sought-after qualities include character, experience, personality, and sufficient work history. These are qualities a leader wants in all personnel, whether they are in the managerial staff or the basic labor force of the organization. Some of these desired qualities are:

Attitude

An attitude is a predisposition to behave or act in a particular way under a given set of circumstances.

This behavior can be positive or negative, but the organization is expecting the behavior to be positive. A person who may be expected to demonstrate a negative attitude could be the person who becomes the "bad apple" who influences the work force in a negative direction in areas in contrast with the expected behavior of the organization.

Enthusiasm

The root word has a spiritual connotation, and suggests connection to a "god which produces an inspired behavior." Any company would welcome an enthusiastic person to their work force. The ability to be eager about a task, or passionate about a product, or zeal in presenting a service is normally considered a positive virtue for an employee. Intense or eager interest in the work to be perform is an asset. If one does not have enthusiasm for a product or service, it probably will not be done well.

Determined

Having one's mind made up, being resolute or firm is a desired quality. To have unwavering loyalty to a company or a "brand" is considered an employable individual. A determined person can bring a single-minded resolve to accomplishing their assigned task. A determined person may suggest a worker that could be a long-time employee. This is good!

Hopefully this will be in favor of the enterprise where you are working.

Motivated

A motivated person has a "motive" a reason or desire for something and also they want a place to "act" on that motive. If a company becomes a place where a person believes their action will fulfill their motive, then the company has a worthy employee. To have inner drive or impulse that causes one to act, or the incentive to behave in the best interests of an enterprise becomes a major asset to the work force.

Confident

Any member of a labor force with confidence in company and themselves becomes a major asset to a company. This person is positive and secure within themselves and self-assured person is a great addition to any staff. To be reliant and have self-confidence in one's own abilities is an advantage to any employee base.

Optimistic

To remain hopeful and positive in a troubled world is a desired quality any leader would be pleased to add to the work force. A belief that good will overcome evil is optimistic and normally makes an individual cheerful. This person becomes a worthy addition to a staff.

Dedicated

To be devoted and committed to a company is a desirable quality in an employee. One who shows dedication and faithfulness to a company is a devoted worker and an asset to a labor force.

Happy

A member of the work force who is contented and pleased with the company and the people with whom they work will also be pleased to promote the product or service they produce.

A cheerful worker spreads happiness throughout the company. This is a good thing!

Listener

Listening is the highest level of hearing. One may hear words without giving any regard to those words. Others may hear and be able to repeat back the exact words, but still do not know what the words mean. Listening requires both analysis and action. A staff person or an employee who will listen becomes a major advocate for the company and one who is willing to communicate company policy to other workers. Such a worker is a rare and precious jewel and should be greatly appreciated by both leadership and management.

Patient

The ability to endure hardships or trouble without complaining is a noble quality. An employee who stands up under pressure and is tolerant of things they cannot control is a desirable member of the labor force. Such a person is capable of enduring circumstances; such as, a work slow-down, union difficulties, economic slump, and be ready for work when the company needs them. Patient people are hard to find, but to add them to the work force would be a desirable addition.

These qualities will be present to varying degrees in most organizational personnel. Hopefully, these qualities are present in the organization where you work.

The Right People in the Right Job

In reality the best approach is have the right plan, using the right people, working on the right problem. Some tasks require exacting detail work while other tasks may be accomplished in less than precise accuracy. However, the only one I can think of is "chopping wood" where there is no required exactness. Also, another task that may fall in this category is janitorial services. However, if "cleanliness is next to godliness" perhaps janitorial services should be excluded also. These two classifications of workers have been given titles: the *Time Teller* and the *Watch Builder*.

All who seek additions to a labor force should be aware of these classifications. When asked the time,

1. A *Time Teller* will give you the time in terms of "about" "almost" or any approximate time.

2. *Watch Builders* are exact people who will give you the correct or exact time.

Those in charge of hiring must match the worker with the job. Never hire a *Time Teller* for exacting detail work. *Watch Builders* are best to have in the labor force. Why? Even seemly unimportant tasks may require exactness. Let the *Time Tellers* chop wood; hire the *Watch Makers*.

When Change Happens

There are key factors that must be present for a change to work:

1. There must be a strong leader to initiate change.
2. Be sure people understand that the need for change is greater than their reasons for resistance to change.

3. A vision that explains the outcomes from the change will facilitate change.
4. Have commitment from the key persons who must be involved to make the change.
5. It is easier to change when change is expected.
6. Measurable benchmarks assist with monitoring progress toward change.
7. A plan in place for follow through is a way to ensure on-going commitments to the change.
8. Once change happens most people will resist going back to the former way of doing a task.
9. Identifying a benefit will assist the acceptance of proposed change.

Workers Expectations in Staff

- One that is honest.
- One that shows appreciation for the work they perform.
- One who shows respect to workers.
- One who listens respectfully to workers.
- One who talks with them and honors their concerns.

What People Do Not Want in Staff

- One filled with self-importance who perceive themselves as above any of the rules.
- One unwilling to appreciate achievement of workers.
- One who abuses the staff.
- One who lays blame on the workers.
- One who shows partiality toward some workers.
- One who pits workers against each other.

Meet With Your People

- Remember, the last two generations were taught that nothing was absolutely wrong or absolutely right.
- Young people growing up now do not have a clear idea about standards.
- These facts color all meetings which deal with problems.
- Huddle spontaneously to handle quick fixes to problems as they arise.
- Meet daily only if the meeting relates to doing that day's work.
- Meet weekly only if there is something major happening that cannot wait.
- Meet monthly or quarterly to review project progress or results. This is a good time to assess team progress.

> *...have the right plan, using the right people, working on the right problem.*

IV

PRACTICAL WORK APPLICATIONS

These practical work applications are for the most part what the author has used in his years as a faith-based leader.

Management by Walking Around

This kind of management is just what it says: as a manager walks around the facility, they get to know the people.

Never walk the same route. Rarely should a worker be corrected on the spot if they are doing something wrong. At the appropriate time, inform the area manager and let him correct the individual. The individual working directly for a manager does not interfere with the manager's authority.

During a walk around, a worker doing an outstanding job may be identified. Send that individual a note of recognition. (Always send a copy of the note to the individual's manager.)

Generally people appreciate being told they are performing well.

One method of managing is to rank people that are the best performers. In the future others will seek to be on the list. There are several reasons why their performance will improve. Having the attention of leadership, they will have the motivation to perform better.

Another application is placing your people into three groups: the loyalists, the herd, and the "why" group. The Loyalists are the people who do their best for the company. The Herd is a group that normally does what supervision wants them to do. The "Why" group always asks questions and want to know the "why" of any new task.

The Loyalists usually are about 10% of workers. The Herd is usually about 80% of the work force. Usually, the "Why" group is about 10% of the labor force. If numbers vary a lot from these percentages there will be problems. For example, if you have too many workers in the "Why" group the result could be a climate of chaos that disrupts production.

Dealing with Gossip

Gossip mongers are those people who maliciously spread gossip, rumor, or hearsay that is negative in nature. This does not include the informal grapevine that is present in all organizations.

The gossip monger intentionally spreads gossip that is harmful to people in the organization or to the organization itself. Dealing with a gossip monger should be handled by a manager, not a leader. If a leader has evidence of a gossip monger, the information should be given to the manager of the gossip monger for action. Often a gossip monger will claim to be innocent.

Regardless of whether one admits to gossiping, the manager should make clear that a repeat performance would produce a termination from the company. Human beings have sufficient difficulties without a gossiper stirring the pot.

Dealing with Conflict

Ask those who disagree to paraphrase the other's comments. This can help them find out if they really understand one another. Are they communicating with one another? Work out a compromise between the persons who have the conflict. Get them to agree on the underlying source of the conflict. Ask each person to list what the other side should do. Have the people on each side make a list of ten questions for their opponents. This will allow them to learn their major concerns about the other's position. The answers may lead them to a compromise. Exchange lists and select a compromise that all are willing to accept. Then have them engage in a give and take discussion until they come to an agreed solution. It is best not to use the words "always," "never," or "ever."

Test the compromise to ensure that it will support the team's goals. Convince team members that sometime they have to admit that they have been wrong. You can help them save face if you can convince them that changing a position may show strength.

Dealing with Meetings

Do not compete with the workers. Let them express their ideas first before you express your views. Listen to everyone. You can paraphrase but do not judge. Do not put anyone on the defensive. Assume that everyone's ideas have value.

Control the dominant people, but do not alienate them. Realize that your interest and alertness are contagious to the group. Keep all people informed about where they are and what is expected of them. It helps to put the ideas on a flip chart that everyone can see. Check with the person in the group who owns the problem if a proposed solution is satisfactory. At times give others a chance at running the meeting.

Another approach, if you need everyone's ideas, is letting the person who is not heard from very often express his ideas first. Work your way up the group, but let the dominate person or persons express their ideas last. Often if the dominate person speaks first, the others will just go along with his ideas and you will not get the true ideas of everyone in the group.

Appraisals

Each company must have some system of appraising the work force. Evaluation should be tied to the goals for the project. Some states require at least an annual appraisal or review of personnel, products and services.

Whether appraisals are made on a monthly, quarterly, semi-annual, or annual basis is up to you. The annual appraisal tends to be just a record keeping requirement. It is best to do the appraisal each quarter and make it a teaching tool for your people.

If a worker does not get a good appraisal, then do a monthly update to see if the person is improving. If no improvement is observed it might be time to consider termination. If that is the case, you have the documentation required in the states that require such documentation for a termination. If you are in an "at will" state, you are free to terminate that person. It is good to have the documentation to reduce your cost of unemployment compensation.

There are a number of commercial employee appraisal forms available, or you may want to design a form for your enterprise to use. Whether you use a commercial form or design your own form, there are a number of factors to be considered:

1. Quality of work
2. Consistency of performance
3. Job knowledge
4. Cooperativeness
5. Initiative
6. Attitude
7. Attention to safety
8. Punctuality and attendance
9. Judgment

There are other factors you may want to consider:

- Some appraisals are done by the immediate supervisor only. You might want to consider also having a self-appraisal as well. This method makes it easier when discussing the appraisals with the person.
- You will note that most people rate themselves lower than the supervisor. However, there are exceptions, particularly when the person is not performing well.

Prepare for the appraisal interview: This is often given little thought or preparation. That is a mistake.

- Notify the person (in writing) of the time and place of the appraisal interview. This should be several days in advance of the meeting.
- Provide the person with a blank copy of the appraisal form.
- If you have self-evaluations, include instructions about filling out the form. Have the person bring the form with them.
- The person doing the appraisal will fill out the form with as much factual information available. Information obtained from the personnel office and other supervisors is helpful.

The appraisal interview: Getting started can be one of the most difficult parts of the interview. It is up to the interviewer to assist the person being interviewed to overcome his initial nervousness.

- Try to have an open, friendly approach so there will not be a angry defensive reaction to the interview. Sometimes this is not possible. Some interviewers think it is best to have some small talk before starting the interview.

- You need to tell the person why the interview is taking place (even if both of you know). Tell the person how the interview will take place.

Your person's self-assessment: This will allow valuable input by your employee. As you read the self-assessment, ask the employee to clarify any comments that you do not understand.

The appraiser's assessment: This is where you will describe the person's performance over the time period that has been set for the assessment.

- You will have discussions about the strengths and weakness you have observed. Differences between the self-assessment and your assessment will be noted and be discussed later.

- Some appraisers will address the strengths first, then address the weaknesses.

- You will then set some goals or action plans to work on toward the end if the interview. You might want to have an action plan worksheet available. You will have a copy and the person will have a copy.

- Some items to keep in mind: Avoid attacking the person. Offer reassurance wherever possible. Restate the person's comments to be sure you understand his comments.
- When the person is talking, do not interrupt except to ask for clarification.

Maslow's Hierarchy of Needs: You might want to review Maslow's *Hierarchy of Needs* and get a feel for where your person is in the hierarchy.

Primary Needs:

Physiological Needs
Food & Housing
Safety

Secondary Needs:

Social
Esteem
Self-Actualization

Maslow's hierarchy has to do with what motivates a person. He stated when a person's need is satisfied we have another need. Needs that are satisfied do not motivate a person. Only those needs that are unsatisfied motivate a person.

Physiological Needs: These are very basic needs such as food, water, air, and rest. These needs must be satisfied in order to survive; they will take precedence over all other needs.

Safety Needs: When the first level of needs is satisfied the next level of needs comes into play, the need for safety and security. A person needs to be safe from harm and have security. A person tries to gain security where they work. One has to have the known rather than the unknown. If you lost your job your need for safety and security would be strong. As soon as possible you would have to have another job to satisfy this need.

These two needs, physiological and safety are primary needs and if these two needs are not fulfilled a person has a lot difficulty coping in the world.

Social Needs: Social needs are desires for acceptance, love, and belonging. This need, knowing one is cared for, is a strong motivator.

Esteem Needs: There are two types of esteem needs, 1. the need for <u>self esteem</u> and 2. the need to gain <u>esteem from others</u>. Self-esteem needs are self-confidence, feeling knowledgeable, and feeling independent and free. Esteem from others needs are reputation, status, appreciation, and respect.

Self-Actualization Needs: Self actualization is a very personal need that varies from person to person. It is a feeling of self-fulfillment, of having realized our potential.

- These three needs, social, esteem, and self-actualization are secondary needs. Some people will not reach this level, or may not go beyond the social need.

- Satisfying these needs does not remain static. People can move from one level to another quickly particularly if going down

a level. People can be at different levels depending upon the circumstances. One may be at a different level at work than perhaps at church.
- The point is that every person experiences these needs.
- Maslow added self-transcendence to his list of needs. Self-transcendence is to connect to something beyond the ego or to help others find self-fulfillment and realize their full potential.

Sensitivity Training

I recommend that you consider learning about Sensitivity Training for yourself and perhaps some of your key people. Learn more by contacting Education Research, PO Box 4205, Warren, N. J. 07060. The ability to "read" people and predict their behavior can be improved.

Human beings have sufficient difficulties without a gossiper stirring the pot.

V

Selecting the People

Some Methods of Selection

It can be simple; use the *Time Teller* method concerning a person you want to do detailed work (discussed in Chapter III). <u>This should be only one item of the selection process.</u> You will need to know a lot more about the person you are considering hiring.

Identify Those Who are "Gifted"

Being "gifted" is not always a result of high intelligence alone. A person that is "gifted" experiences exceptional psychological, spiritual, and intellectual development.

A "gifted" person is well on their way to self-actualization, by exhibiting the following personality traits:

Information Processing

This includes unique perceptions and awareness of their own environment, sense of humor and creativity, questioning and searching for the truth, insightfulness, comfortable with both divergent and synergistic thinking, also very curious and with a creative drive. They are more process oriented than product oriented. They hold divergent values compared to mainstream culture.

High Sensitivity

Sensitivity toward other people is often connected with a sense of alienation from other people and the person feels lonely. He is aware of the complexities of life and the consequences of his actions. He has an acute awareness of the expectations of other people.

Intensity

He has a high energy level, emotional reactivity, and high arousal of the central nervous system.

Multiple Interests

Having capabilities in many areas, he can easily move from on pursuit to another, and has the ability to handle many things at once.

Realistic

He strives for moral integrity, is interested in social serve, has high standards, and has low tolerance for mediocrity and frustration.

Perfectionist

Self-critical, he labels himself as scattered, and has a low tolerance of making mistakes. Regarding failure he thinks he is more to blame than other people and finds it difficult to take credit for his achievements or abilities.

Need For Autonomy

He has feelings of being out of step with other people, and may experience deep conflicts between his need for self-actualization and maintaining traditional relationships.

Intense Moral Commitment

If he sees injustice he will attempt to do something about it. He is willing to stand up for his beliefs. He has a respect for all human beings. He has a greater capacity and concern for others, especially children. .

*

You may or may not see all of these gifted traits in people you seek for employment or people that are already working for you.

When you are interviewing someone for employment you will want to make a good first impression. You must gain strong eye contact with that person in a way that shows you are interested in what she has to say.

Listener

Do you often find yourself not hearing others as they intend you to hear them? When you really want to listen to a person, you do not want to be a mind reader. Do not dwell on what you think a person is really thinking or feeling. Also do not think strongly on what you are going to say.

Do not have selective listening where you only hear what you want to hear. You may agree with what is being said just to be nice and avoid conflict.

You may ask a potential employee "If I met your former boss and asked to hear one sentence about you, what would that one sentence be? Chances are he will give you an accurate picture of that person.

*

If you have flextime benefits tell the candidate and be sure he understands. You might give his a list of those benefits.

*

Find out the job candidates reading speed. There is evidence that the faster you read and understand what you are reading, the greater the candidate's learning ability. The better the learning ability, the faster he will learn the job. You can develop a reading test that can be read easily. Have questions so you will know if they understood.

*

You can learn a lot about a job applicant by asking his response to a practical, but what would be a tough situation. Tell him a client called and said we had messed up his order and he may lose a customer. Tell him because you are tied up you want the job applicant to write a response in fifteen minutes. If I like it I will send it to the client. This exercise will give you more information about the applicant than just his resume or the interview alone.

VI

Troubleshooting

A Basic Task

A basic task of leadership and managerial staff is to find and eliminate problems that may hinder the personnel, production or services of an organization. When problems and identified the process leads to mediation. This includes arbitration, negotiation, and intervention to resolve conflict. Achieving agreement in areas that are problematic is the defining ingredient in leadership.

The General Checklist

Whenever you have a management problem, these are general steps you should take to solve it successfully.

1. State the problem specifically in terms of Its source (who is responsible for causing the problem not who is responsible to fix the problem.)
2. The kind of problem it is; (a performance or behavior problem, etc.)
3. Ask questions and gather facts you need to make a decision.
4. Identify the options available to you for solving the problem, now that you know exactly what the problem is.
5. Choose an option that you will follow or a series of steps if that is the best way.

6. Consider writing down the reasons why you chose the option you did, particularly if you will have to defend your actions later.
7. Act by implementing your decision.
8. Evaluate how well your decision worked.

Checklist One: Performance Problems.

Answer each of these questions:

1. Exactly what is the nature of the performance problem?
2. Does the employee have basic self management skills such as skill in organizing work as setting priorities and meeting deadlines?
3. Does the employee have the technical work skills needed to complete his assignments? If not, arrange to get him the training for these skills.

If the employee is still not able to do the work after additional training you have two options.

1. Transfer him to a different job that you think he can do.
2. Terminate employment.

Checklist 2: Conduct/Behavior Problems

Answer the following questions:

1. What is the unacceptable behavior by the employee?
2. Is the behavior serious or merely irritating?

If it is merely irritating tell the employee his conduct is not acceptable and you may take stronger measures if the behavior does not improve.

3. Be prepared to live with most irritations unless it gets worse or is interfering with productivity.
4. Does the employee know the rules he has to follow?

If not, let the employee know what the rules are and that all workers are expected to follow the rules. If not, there will be other consequences for not following the rules. Make a written record of the warning.

5. Is the behavior critical to safety or to the well-being of other people?

If so your first action is to see the behavior is stopped. Decide the penalty for the misbehavior.

If it is serious terminate the employee unless there are mitigating circumstances.

6. Does the behavior undermine your authority?

If so terminate the employee.

Checklist 3: Acceptance Problems.

1. What problem is occurring?
2. Are others failing to accept a worker because she is a woman or a minority group?

If so make sure your people know the company's policy on discrimination. Make sure they know the federal rules on discrimination and that the company could be in serious legal trouble if this continues.

3. Are other people failing to accept an individual simply because he irritates them?

Encourage your employees to work together harmoniously. It can be a part of your performance appraisal.

Checklist 4: Problems with your boss:

Answer these questions:

1. What problem is your boss causing you?
2. Is it a problem that will harm the company, harm you, or something requiring you to something immoral or illegal?
3. If it is not one of these, why is it a problem?

It seems to be a disagreement. This means you should try to persuade your boss to do otherwise. If you cannot persuade him then do what he wants.

4. Does he want you to do something that will harm you, such as hurt your career or make you look bad?

If so, and you trust your boss, discuss it with him. If you are not satisfied with the results of the discussion, decide to live with it or if it is that important to you look for work elsewhere.

Checklist 5: Your personal problems

Answer these questions:

1. What is the problem?
2. Is your boss dissatisfied with you or unhappy with you?

If so talk to your boss about what he wants to see changed. If it something you can fix, fix it. If it something you cannot fix or are unwilling to change, you must know the boss will come out the winner. Look for another job or be prepared to live with the problem.

3. Are personal problems interfering with your work?

Talk to your boss about the problems you are having. Try to work out some temporary accommodations that are acceptable to both of you, until you solve the problems.

Do not keep it to yourself. Your boss may think you have lost interest in your job.

4. Are you burned out on the job?

If so try to find an interest either on the job or your personal life that will revitalize you. If possible you may want to take some time off. to relax and reassess your situation of where you are what you want to be doing.

Checklist 6: Substance abuse problems:

A growing concern is the impact of alcohol or drug abuse on employee productivity. Costs that may be hidden results from poor quality work, absenteeism, personal conflicts and other factors.

Change:
- In an employee's behavior.
- In an employee's patterns of work and absences.
- In the way an employee relates to others.
- In the quality of an employee's work.
- In the amount of work the employee produces.

Sometimes you can be able to identify impaired employees by physical symptoms:
- The odor of alcohol.
- Dilated pupils.
- Slurred or incoherent speech.
- Disorientation.
- Lack of muscular coordination.

Testing methods are available to determine drug abuse; however testing must be on all employees which can be expensive. When an employee tests positive you can send him to a rehabilitation program. When he tests negative you can require him to be tested routinely.

VII

Supervising

Three Levels

In most enterprises there are three levels of management:

- Leadership
- Managerial oversight
- Supervising.

The Leader is the CEO of the enterprise. The Manager is the head of a department in the enterprise. The Supervisor is the head of a section within the department. Yet, all leadership positions relate to the function of supervising.

In reality, supervising includes observing, serving, directing, problem-solving, and dealing with difficult situations. These are the general and specific functions of everyone in an oversight position.

The purpose of this portion is to assist an individual being considered for a supervisor position to understand both the functionality of supervising and how their work life would change should they move into the arena of the supervisor. As a supervisor one would be associating with the upper level of the organization as well as middle management and at times with the entire labor force.

Dealings with these levels of leadership will require continued growth and improvement. There is no rest for the weary. Workers are frequently able to find a niche or place to hide, but those in a supervisory role cannot hide.

On the positive side, supervisors almost always know what is happening in the organization.

As part of the managerial team, supervisors attend meetings, receive written information and are frequently consulted. Supervisors have a deeper feeling of involvement with the organization. This provides an opportunity to contribute to the welfare of the work force. As part of the team, supervisors can go to bat for those who are deserving counseling workers who have lost their courage, and those whose outlook has become negative

Disadvantages of Supervising

Problem employees can be difficult. Expect to be more alone as a supervisor. You may become isolated to some extent from the people you supervise. It is impossible to be a supervisor and a close friend at the same time. This feeling of being alone will happen when you make an unpopular decision and your people let you know you are on the opposite side of the fence. You may not receive constant reinforcement from those above you.

Being a supervisor will probably mean more work hours than you did as a worker. You may have to take some of your extra work home. Should you decide to become a supervisor, understanding the prior image predominance theory will assist you.

When you became a supervisor those above you may have an image built on first impressions.

After you have been with your organization for a while you become more confident that you are competent in your job. A prior image based on first impressions is no longer fair to you. You may need to make a special effort on how you are now performing will change the prior image. Your goal now is that everyone will sense you new maturity and will not treat you unfairly because of your prior image.

There are some questions at this point you should ask yourself. Is the price of becoming a supervisor too high? As a supervisor you may be as happy as the people you supervise?

Becoming a Supervisor

If you become a supervisor, your first step will be to keep your eyes wide open, and as quickly as possible get the lay of the land in your new position. There are situations you need to know about as quickly as possible:

- Are you inheriting some sensitive human relations circumstances?
- Will you have any problem people?
- Are there differences in leadership style between yourself and your predecessor?
- Are there any unusual protocols?
- Are there any informal reports you need to know about?

- Upon what criteria will you be evaluated?

It is one thing to learn about management theory - it is another thing to put that knowledge into practice. Your first few weeks are most critical. When you become a supervisor, try the suggestions that follow:

- Use your new power in a sensitive manner.
- Be patient with yourself.
- Decide to be a professional person.
- Stay in contact with your people.
- Make changes gradually.
- Watch the upside (those above you), while protecting your downside (those people who work for you).

Save Some Time For Planning

- Redefine your working relationships with people who work for you.
- Let your people help you.
- Adopt a learning attitude.

Initial Goals As A Supervisor

- Keep the productivity and efficiency of your section at the same levels with some improvements if possible.

- Start building a new strong relationship with your people. Also start building a strong relationship with your fellow supervisors.
- Make progress in becoming a solid member of the management team.
- No matter how you feel on the inside, stay positive and confident of the outside.
- Be careful not to create more problems than you solve.

Getting Productivity Through Your People

You will get productivity by working with your people. You no longer do the work yourself:

- Train your people and have them do it.
- You are responsible for the work done by your people.
- You must learn to take personal satisfaction in working with your people.
- Only through the individual productivity of all your people will you create the productivity of your section.

Your work as a supervisor can be defined as planning, organizing, directing, coordinating, and controlling the work in your section to achieve productivity goals in your section.

Motivation Techniques

You may have a person working for you that has an excellent productivity record.. Suddenly that high productivity drops down. The supervisor may want to give the person a few days to bounce back without interference. But when too much time has passed and there is no improvement, you will want to find out what the problem is. You want to discover the cause and take immediate steps to bring the persons productivity back up. If the cause is something on the job it will be easier to do than if the cause is something off the job.

Communication failures and damaged ego's are common in many circumstances. You must be alert to drops in productivity. You cannot always wait to find out if the problem is job related or not.

All drops in productivity are not sudden. Frequently the drop is gradual. In this circumstance the cause is more difficult to determine if at all.

You can improve motivation by giving some of your people special assignments, rotating jobs if possible, or be providing some special learning opportunities. Everything you do as a supervisor can have an impact on your people.

Management books are full of theories on how to motivate your people. An example world be the "Hawthorne Experiments" conducted by the Western Electric Company from 1927 to 1932.

Western Electric found that no matter what improvements were made production increased. Why? The group felt special and just making improvements gave them more status and respect. These studies proved that the emotional climate of the workers is important.

Many psychologists claimed that inner needs must be satisfied before the workers can reach their full potential. A primary need is physiological such as hunger. A secondary need is one that satisfies the mind or ego.

"Maslow's Hierarchy of Needs" (discussed in Chapter IV) became the most popular in determining needs priority.

Primary (or basic) Needs:

The first level of need is physiological, food good health.

The second level is safety/security, out of danger.

Secondary Needs:

The third level is social needs/love/belonging. One needs to be accepted and enjoy the company of others.

The fourth level is esteem/ego needs. To achieve, be competent, gain approval, and recognition from others.

The fifth level is cognitive. To know, to understand, and explore.

The sixth level is aesthetic. To know symmetry, order, and beauty.

The seventh level is self actualization. One has self-fulfillment, and you realize one's potential.

The eighth level is self-transcendence. To connect to something beyond the ego, or to help others find self-fulfillment and realize their potential.

The need at the bottom must be fulfilled before the next one can be fulfilled. *Your people's first three needs are probably satisfied, so concentrate on the ego and self-fulfillment needs.*

For achieving increased productivity you need to keep the following principles in mind:

- The technical skills you have are important because you must know the job skills before you can teach your people. If you do not know the job skills you must have someone else with that knowledge teach your people.

- Spending time to restore or improve your relationship with one of your people whose productivity is down is very important. You will have more things to do than you have time. Prioritize the things you have to do. Number one priority should be keeping productivity as high as possible.

- If the productivity of one of people drops, you need to know about it as soon as possible and begin efforts to do something about it.
- Upper management expects you to achieve productivity from your new people in a hurry. Today a faster pay off that was expected in the past. Workers today have a shorter span of employment before they move on. The pace inside most organizations is faster today. Orientation periods have been speeded up with less time being spent on initial training. Training today is more expensive.
- This all means you must build relations with new workers as early as possible. You must train them more quickly so they will reach a good productivity levels in a shorter span of time.
- Your future promotions will be based on the productivity of the people who work for you now. Upper managers will look at many factors, but nothing will make a favorable decision than you having the human relations skill to get productivity from your people. To ignore or underestimate this principle in any way will damage your career.

Build Sound Relationships

- Build relationship with key people first.
- Do not play games with relationships.

- Do not build one relationship at the expense of another.
- Build your relationship with a new hire quickly and carefully.
- Relationships require daily maintenance.
- In addition to building and maintaining good relationships with your people do not neglect your relationships with your fellow supervisors.

Irreplaceable Foundations

You will make a mistake if you take these foundations lightly. If you weave them into your leadership style, your success as a supervisor is more certain.

- Give clear and complete instructions.
- Your people know how they are doing.
- Give credit when credit is due.
- Involve your people in your decisions.
- *Maintain an open-door policy.*

These are foundations you as supervisor can use in building and keeping healthy relationships with your people.

Write out the foundations on a wallet-sized card so you can keep them in your wallet. Memorize these foundations and start practicing them right away.

*Do not play games
with relationships.*

VIII

BUSINESS LAW

Where does our law come from?

United States law consists of:
**Black letter law and
Common law**

Black letter law has two divisions. The first division is the laws passed by congress and the state legislatures. The second division is the rules and regulations made by the administrative agencies of both the congress and state legislatures. Their rules and regulations are considered black letter law.

Common law is rulings of the courts that have the effect of creating law for that court's jurisdiction. Common law, in effect, is judge-made law.

If it has been appealed to the US Supreme Court and is upheld by that court, it then becomes the common law for the entire nation.

Black letter law supersedes the common law unless the Supreme Court declares the black letter law unconstitutional. Business law is a mixture of black letter law and common law.

Contract Law

Simply put a contract is an agreement between two or more parties. The contract can be oral or written. When the contract is important it can be put in writing. We make many oral contracts daily. For example when you agree to buy bread in a store, you have an oral contract.

Contract law comes from the common law. However it may be black letter law if it is on a topic that is covered by the Uniform Commercial Code (UCC) which has been adopted by all the states, or any other law adopted.

A contract has four elements that are required. These are 1. mutual assent; 2. consideration; 3. legality of the subject matter; and 4. capacity of the persons to enter into contracts.

Mutual assent is where the parties agree. This usually where on party makes an offer and the other party accepting that offer.

Consideration is something given or promised to bind the agreement. This can be money or something of value   For example, a promise to do something that they were not required to do is sufficient.

Legality of the subject matter simply means that the subject matter must be legal. For example you could not make a contract to rob a store.

Capacity of one of the parties means that they cannot be underage, insane or otherwise legally incapacitated. If so the contract can be voided.

Offer

An offer may be defined as a definite conditional undertaking. An offer is always a promise to do something in return for someone doing an act or a promise to do an act.

This offer must be distinguished from a mere invitation for someone to make an offer. An offer must define the subject matter and set forth terms such as quantity and price.

Acceptance

The offer is only one part on the mutual assent the other is acceptance. The person making the offer has complete power to cancel the offer before it is accepted. If the offer sets a time for the offer to be accepted and that time is not met the offer is canceled. The offer may specify the manner it is to be accepted. An example would be that it must be in writing. If that is not done the offer is void.

Mutual assent required both an offer and an acceptance. Acceptance is some overt act by which indicates assent.

Remember those who make an offer may ask those who receive the offer to accept by giving a return promise or by doing an act. When it calls for a promise it is a bilateral contract. When it calls for doing an act it is a unilateral contract. An acceptance of an offer must generally be positive and clear.

Consideration

Consideration means that something must be given by each of the parties in the contract to bind the parties in the contract.. The parties must have intended the exchange as consideration for the contract.

What is given must be either a benefit or a detriment to the promise.

A minor who sells property to another can immediately disaffirm and recover the property. But, if the buyer has already transferred the property to another and if the third party has no knowledge of the purchase from a minor, the minor cannot get the property back.

The Statue of Frauds

All contracts are enforceable with the exception of:

- A promise of an executor to answer for the debts of a decedent.
- A promise to answer for the debt of another.
- A promise where marriage is the consideration.
- A sale of any interest in land.
- A contract that cannot be performed in one year.
- A sale of goods for $500.00 or more.

The Parole Evidence Rule

If it is claimed that the parties had not really agreed to what was written in the contract, but something understood before the signing, if that something was an option to change his mind under certain circumstances.

The parole evidence rule prevents any change of the written contract. Points to remember in regard to the parole evidence rule:
- The rule applies only when there is a fully written contract.
- The rule excludes only evidence occurring before or at the signing of the contract.
- Only evidence that changes the terms of the written contract is excluded.

Discharge of Contracts

How do parties to a contract become free of the contract? If the parties have performed their obligations as required by the contract they are discharged.

Some contracts are made subsequent to a condition happening. If that condition does not happen the parties are discharged. Such a condition does not happen that condition is called a condition precedent. If the condition requires something to be performed, that condition is called a condition subsequent, because it occurs after the performance of the duties required.

Discharge of the contract has a number of options:
- Performance of the duties required.

- One party may breach the contract.
- All parties may rescind the contract.
- One party may be substituted for another is an ovation.
- A voidable contract may be avoided by a minor, a mentally incompetent person, or by reason of fraud or duress.
- The subject matter of the contract may become   illegal.
- There may be objective impossibility.
- There may be discharge in bankruptcy.
- There may be a statute of limitations that will discharge the obligations.

Assignments

- Personal rights cannot be transferred to other people.

- Property rights can be transferred to other people.
- Contract duties are not assignable. A party may delegate duties to another person but the original party must perform the duties if the delegate does not.

Agency Law

An agent is someone who represents another person contractually. The person represented is called the principle.

When the agent acts within the scope of his authority the principle is bound by the contract made on his behalf.

A husband or wife is not the agent of the other spouse.

Remember, there are people who add ifs, ands, or buts to the law and leave the law open to the interpretation of each person's faulty conscience and perception of right and wrong.

IX

Administrative Potpourri

How To Shut Down A Motor Mouth

Keep silent. Any oral response, even sounds like "um" and "un huh," will bring about more chatter. Keep the "motor mouth" feeling self-conscious through total silence.

Speak at a very slow tempo. Most motor mouths are fast talkers.

Create a contrast. By doing this you want him to think hopefully that he is talking too much.

Never restate what you hear from a "motor mouth." If you do and you are correct, they will say something like " Yes, you are right," then repeat what was said. If you are wrong, the "motor mouth" will talk twice as much and faster.

Say "Goodbye!" when the "motor mouth" is through.

The Careful Critic

No one likes to be told they have done something wrong. You need to be able to correct someone without it destroying that person.

Say nothing until you determine how it will affect that person's self-interest. Express your opinion in terms of how it will affect that person's goals on the job.

If presenting your criticism directly is not appropriate, try these approaches:

Ask for clarification. Let the individual work through his flaws Then include his flaws in a statement such as, "If I have got this straight" summary.

Solicit questions. Get the individual to think of his inadequacies. Keep your voice neutral.

Fill in the picture. Anyone can make faulty decisions if he has limited knowledge of the situation.

Shifts the blame. When a person does that, make sure he understands how the other individuals feel about the situation. Do not let the individual believe he is never wrong.

Character Flaws

Are you too trusting? Be concerned about people with the following character flaws.

- People who rarely do what they say they will do.
- People who push their work onto someone else.
- People who are late and do not apologize or explain.
- People who say, "I am too busy."
- People who reject your ideas out of hand.

- People who will not help you when you are in a jam.

Promise Keepers Findings About Men

- Many men are mostly friendless. They feel themselves relationally isolated. It is difficult for such men to have deep, lasting relationships.
- Men are emotionally isolated. For most men, other than expressing anger, it is very difficult to share their emotions, to cry, or express that they have a need.
- Men are confused about their masculinity. It is important to direct men toward what is good about manhood, including integrity, courage and the ability to share with other men.
- Men are success driven. The search for doing good at work often means that it comes as a cost to their home life.
- Pastors and church leaders are usually very isolated. They are without the friendship and accountability that is so necessary for a healthy manhood.

Keys To Successful Leadership

- Maintain absolute integrity.
- Know your subject matter.

- Declare your vision for your company.
- Show uncommon commitment.
- Expect positive results by turning disadvantages into advantages.
- Take care of your people.
- Put duty before self.
- Find out what the business wants for returns.

The Essence OF Good Decisions

- Great decisions come from saying "I do not know."
- Deciding is not about consensus.
- Great decisions come from knowing the external factors.
- Hugh decisions decide only a tiny fraction of the outcome.
- Think long term such as the next quarter-century not the quarter of the year.
- You can make big mistakes and still prevail.

Beware These Flaws In People

- Professes to be able to work with anybody.
- Name drops.
- Makes unrealistic claims.
- Talks about himself more than anyone else.

- Pressures you for a commitment.

You will probably have these people working for you. Hopefully not all of them.

People You Might Have Working for You

- The know it all!
- The passive person!
- The dictators!
- The "yes" people!
- The "no" people!
- The gripers!

As you gain experience you will learn to understand the difficult people in your workgroup. You will learn what to do or say to these people. You will then become less of a target.

Discrimination

Can you spot discrimination in your business? There can be legal consequences if you cannot. Creating a policy that protects people who report discrimination protects you legally.

If no one complains when they witness discriminatory behavior, does that not get you off the legal hook? A case can be made that you should have known about the person who commits discriminatory behavior.

The contents of email messages by employees are admissible as evidence of discrimination.

Managing Time

- Decide immediately where each paper goes. Do not set aside for a later decision.
- After working with a file put it away before starting another project.
- Be selective about what you save. File things quickly.
- Jot notes in the proper place, not on little pieces of note paper that are easily lost.
- Clear your desk at the end of the day.

If there are a number of projects sitting on your back burner, but you never seem to have the time to get to them:

1. Take each project and write a plan for accomplishing it.
2. Break the project into a number of steps.
3. Identify steps that will take 20 minutes or less to do.
4. Make a commitment to do these steps by scheduling them on your calendar.
5. Be sure to complete one 20 minute step each day.

If you are working at home but keep getting distracted by things around the house that need attention:

1. Act as if you have a conventional job. Set specific work hours.
2. Schedule two hours of work time with 30 minute breaks.
3. During break time you can do things around the house that can be done in 30 minutes.
4. Gather all the items you will need for your work time before you start. This way you will not need to search the home for something you need and get distracted by something else.

Ways to Enjoy Life

- Get away for a weekend.
- Enjoy a nap.
- Take a short walk.
- Delegate chores to others.
- Request help when needed.
- Ask people to respect your limits.
- Set realistic goals and deadlines.
- Offer to help someone else.
- Volunteer to tutor a child.
- Let your people know when they have done something right.

Ways to Discover Your Purpose

- Make a list of your goals.
- Pray for wisdom and insight.
- Take a gift discovery class.
- Ask for opportunities to serve.
- Cultivate an attitude of gratitude.
- Seek more responsibility at work.
- Give of your time, talent and treasures.

Ways to Become a Friend

- Encourage people in their walk with God.
- Ask others for their prayer support.
- Be observant; offer your help when needed.
- Forgive an offense.
- Practice exercising patience toward others.
- Remember how it is to be a newcomer.
- Learn to serve others.

How to Get Organized

- Create a useable filing system.
- Toss junk mail when received.
- Get rid of stuff you no longer need.
- Eliminate clutter in your office.
- Cancel subscriptions you do not read.

- Shred sensitive papers before trashing.
- Collect receipts and put them in order for tax purposes.
- Keep a list of daily goals at your desk.

Memory

1. Commit short term memory items in the morning. Your brain stores short term memory items about 15% better in the morning.
2. Commit long term memory items in the afternoon.
3. Want to remember something you read? These memory tips help:
   - What was it about?
   - What parts of it were important?
   - What opinions if any did it contain?
   - What is your opinion of the article?
   - What makes it unique?

Leaders

See if you possess these qualities of a true leader:

- Leaders start projects with "What has to be done?" not "What do I want?"
- Leaders next ask, "What do I have to do to make a real contribution?"

- Leaders continually ask, "What are the goals and objectives of my organization?"
- Leaders do not want clones of themselves as employees. They never ask, " Do I like or dislike this employee?"
- Leaders are not threatened by others who have strong points they lack.

Ways to Build a Top Staff

- Be friendly with staff members, but do not treat them as best friends.
- Tell them everything they need to know and expect the same from your staff.
- Build trust in your staff and they will build trust in you.
- Invest heavily in loyalty from your staff, and be loyal to them.
- Fairness on your part establishes your credibility.
- Never be too busy to laugh with your people.

Proper Delegation Builds Team Spirit

- Pick people who can accept responsibility. Try to match the person to the job.
- Build people's confidence by assigning low priority tasks in the beginning.

- Keep tabs on what you delegate. As the deadline nears, check to make sure everything is on target.

Ways to Help You Solve a Problem.

- Call attention to your typed letters by adding a P.S. in your handwriting. It is the first thing the reader will notice.
- Periodically, take your to do list and ask yourself "If I had only 30 more days on the job, which tasks would I want to do before I leave?" You will quickly identify the top priority tasks.
- At the end of a meeting do not ask, "What else do we have to discuss?" Instead, try, "Is there something I can put on the agenda for the next meeting?" You will prevent dragging out this meeting and the people will have something to think about before the next meeting.

Communicating Better at Work

Understand that communication is a two-way street. It involves you giving information, and wanting good feedback.

- Do not forget, when possible, face-to-face communication is best because you can have feedback. Written communications often get no feedback.

- When you give an instruction, be sure it is clear and understood.
- Listen to employees and show respect for them when they speak.
- Concentrate on building credibility with your people. Ask yourself these questions:
    1. What are we doing?
    2. What should we be doing?
    3. What should we do next?
    4. What should we not be doing?

How to Become a Better Speaker

- Most people should speak more loudly.
- Invest some time in analyzing the audience.
- Tell them something they do not know.
- Avoid reading a speech with your eyes glued to the lectern.
- It is a good idea to videotape your rehearsals.
- Spend three seconds looking directly at as many of the people in the audience as possible.
- Pause instead of uttering "ums" and "ahs."

How to Become a Better Leader/Manager:

- Think big with ideas that will be contagious and excite your people.
- Encourage your people to do their best.
- Set and maintain high expectations with all who work for you.
- Successful managers find the time to say please and thank you.

Information Management

Information provides the means for coordinating every aspect of the business. A management information system provides the information needed for planning, control, and decision making.

Computer systems can provide the information gathering, processing, retrieval and reporting. The system should be designed to provide data, but also to provide data on exceptions.

Decision support systems enable leaders and managers to plan, monitor, and control performance.

Statistical analysis adds a mathematical dimension to management's interpretation and use of information.

Management information systems serve three vital functions:

1. It serves well to report performance and results. Managers can find out how well they and their people have done at any time.

2. It draws attention to problems as quickly as possible after they occur.
3. It provides the data for research and planning.

An effective MIS must be useful, above all other reasons:

- The MIS must be able to be timely.
- The MIS must be affordable.

Major Time Wasters

- Trying to do too many things at once.
- Set priorities.
- Being afraid to delegate.
- Being afraid to say "No."
- Being tied to the phone: Have someone screen your calls.
- Procrastinating: Get the unpleasant tasks done first if they are important.

The Social Readjustment Scale

When you have people that are having problems at work, you may want to question if any of the factors of the Social Readjustment Scale have occurred in their life.

Life events that have occurred are listed below in descending order in regard to their importance:

1. Death of a spouse.

2. Divorce.
3. Marital separation from mate.
4. Death of a close family member.
5. Major injury or illness.
6. Marriage.
7. Marital reconciliation with mate.
8. Major change in health or behavior of a family member.

Anger is Universal

Ask yourself if whatever made you angry is important to you When you get angry:
- Silently tell yourself stop.
- Distract yourself by thinking of something pleasant.
- Breath in, clinch your fist, breath out, and relax.

Approach to Learning and Improvement

1. Identify the problem or process that will be addressed and describe the improvement opportunity.
2. Describe the current process and include the requirements that must be met.
3. Determine what data will be collected and how performance will be measured. Use subject matter experts as necessary.

4. Describe the possible causes of the problem and determine the root causes.
   5. Develop a workable solution and action plan including targets and improvement resources.

People Who Talk To Themselves

They have a captive audience - not competitive. Often they are trying to better themselves. I am constantly talking to myself. When you do this you are coaching yourself. You can give yourself some immediate unfiltered feedback.

Research has revealed that "private speech" starts as soon as kids begin to talk. This serves two purposes. It helps kids learn language skills and it allows them to reflect and understand daily experiences.

Talking to yourself helps you to think. It provides feedback and helps with self-motivation. It is wise to continue talking to yourself throughout your life. Ask yourself, how am I doing? Am I living up to my commitments?

Great success can come with small personal conversations with yourself. Holy Scripture recorded that Nehemiah "took counsel of himself and got good advice."

The Productive Employee

   1. Identify your top ten timewasters.

2. Be proactive instead of reactive.
3. Schedule your day.
4. Stop waking up and being stressed about yesterday.
5. Focus on today.

Stages of Accountability

When you are trying to get your people to become more accountable and you do not know what stage your people are at, it will be difficult to expect them to be more accountable.

People's reactions to the stages of accountability are similar to the patterns following grief. The five stages of accountability are:

1. denial,
2. anxiety,
3. anger,
4. bargaining
5. accountability.

Rules For Success (By Adrian Newman)

Balance: Try your best to balance your life. Your work, your family, and your friends, they should all have your attention.

Goal setting: Set goals, both business and personal. Make them attainable, yet challenging. When you have reached your goals, you will have a sense of accomplishment.

Hard Work: You must move on to your next task. Strive to meet all your goals as hard as you can.

Get Advice: Ask experts questions. Get your answers whether it is from a book or other writings or from a person. Getting an experts opinion is the right way.

Get up early: The more hours you have in a day, the more you can get done. If you get up an hour earlier, you will have seven extra hours a week.

Adapt When Needed: The world is always changing. To succeed and survive, you need to adapt. If there is a need to change that will help you, change. Do not be stubborn to change, it could be your downfall.

Core Beliefs: Keep your core beliefs, they are important. Get on with your life, but retain your core beliefs.

Be Honest: Be honest with people even when they lie about something.

Be Diplomatic and Compassionate: Give someone an honest answer in a kind and gentle manner.

Never Lose Focus: It can be hard for some people to focus on something they are doing. Whatever you are doing keep yourself focused on what you are doing!

Eliminate Fuzzy Thinking Forever

Fuzzy thinking can be a result of lack of focus due to failure to acquire critical information. This can cause failure for your chance of success. Many people are unaware that critical information they need is essential to their success.

To go from fuzzy thinking to focused thinking answer these questions for yourself:

1. What exactly do you want?
2. What is the absolute minimum necessary to have it?
3. What is the fastest and easiest way to get it?

X

Managerial Communications

How Well Do You Think?

Most of us are not aware of the way we think. Research now has indicated that people do think in different ways. The differences account for the way we make decisions, and for the irritation and resentment we feel toward others when they refuse to see things any "sensible" person would.

Research has even put labels on how we think most of the time. These labels are:

1. Synthesis
2. Idealist
3. Pragmatist
4. Analyst
5. Realist.

In regard to communication - if we understand the different ways people think it is easier to realize their reactions to our communications.

Communication in management has become a concern of people who are in managerial positions. We have worked very hard at our communications but often are surprised to find what we have communicated has not been understood in the way we wanted it to.

Communications have been very elusive to us. Part of the problem is the noise level, where it is almost possible to listen with all the babble that is going on. Some of this outside of us, but too often it is occurring within us. Despite the state of communications in practice we have learned quite a bit about communications.

What We Have Learned About Managerial Communications:

We have learned mostly by doing the wrong things. We have learned that:
- Communication is perception.
- Communication is expectation.
- Communication makes demands.

Communication and information are different, and largely opposite, yet interdependent.

Perception

Communication is perception.

There is no sound unless there is someone to hear it. Sound is created by perception. Sound is potential communication

We now know it is the recipient who communicates. The sender who emits the communication does not communicate. He utters what he thinks is communication. Unless there is someone to hear and understand there is no communication. The sender only makes it possible or impossible for a recipient (percipient) to perceive what has been said.

Keep in mind the silent part of language. Gestures, tone of voice, the environment, the cultural and social contest are all a part of the spoken language.

We know about perception that one can perceive what one is capable of perceiving. Just as the ear cannot hear sounds above a certain level, so the mind does not perceive what is beyond its range of perception.

One has to talk to people in terms of their own experience. In communicating you have to ask yourself is what I say within the recipient's range of perception? The most important limitations on perception are cultural and emotional rather than physical.

Expectations

We perceive what we expect to perceive.

We see and hear largely what we expect. The unexpected may be resented. The unexpected is usually not received at all. It is not seen or heard, but ignored. The mind attempts to fit impressions and stimuli into a frame of expectations.

It is possible to alert the human mind that what it perceives is contrary to its expectations. This requires that we understand what it expects to perceive. This then requires that there be a unmistakable realization that this is different. This will reinforce the condition that this will not work. It will rather reinforce expectations. This makes it more certain that what will be perceived is what the recipient expects to perceive.

Before we can communicate, we must know what the recipient expects to see and hear. Only then can we know communication fits into expectations.

Demands

Communication makes demands.

Words are not merely information. They do carry emotional charges. Words with unpleasant or threatening meanings tend to be suppressed. Words with pleasant meanings tend to be retained.

Communication often is propaganda. The sender wants to get something across to the recipient. Propaganda can be very powerful. The danger of propaganda is that it will be believed. There is also the danger that it will not be believed. No communication is received. Anything any one has to say is considered a demand and can be resisted, resented and not heard at all.

Communication almost always makes a demand. It demands that the recipient be somebody, do something, believe something. It always appeals to motivation If the communication fits in with the values and purpose of the recipient, it is powerful. If it goes against them, it is likely not to be received at all.

Why Communications and Information are Different

They are largely opposite and yet interdependent. Communication is perception. Information is logic.

Information is formal. It is impersonal. The more that it can be freed of the human component of emotions and values, expectations, and perceptions the more valid and reliable and informative it becomes.

Now we have the capacity to provide reliable information because of the technical work accomplished on data processing and data storage by computer. We now have the problem of handling information that is devoid of any communication content.

The requirements for effective information is always specific. We perceive a pattern in communication, but we convey specific data in the information process. The fewer data needed the better the information. An overload of information leads to information blackout. It does not enrich but it impoverishes.

This shows that the effectiveness of an information system depends upon the willingness and ability to think through carefully what information is needed by whom and for what purpose. Communication among the various parties as to the specific meaning of each input and output depends on the pre-establishment of communication.

Why Downward Communications Do Not Work

We have long attempted communication downward. This cannot work because no matter how hard we try it assumes that the sender communicates. But communication is the act of the recipient.

All one can communicate downward are commands. Nothing else can be communicated downward that is connected with understanding, let alone motivation. This requires communication upwards, from those who want to perceive to those who want to reach their perception. This does not mean that managers should not be working on clarity. It does mean that how we say something comes only after we have learned what to say.

The manager must know what his people want to perceive. Communication must be based on the recipient's perception rather than the sender's perception.

Listening is a starting point for communication, but it is inadequate by itself. Listening assumes that the manager will understand what he is being told. It is hard to see why the subordinates should do what the superior cannot do. Listening does not take into consideration that communication is demand. It does not bring out the subordinates preferences and desires and aspirations.

The effectiveness of the information process will depend on our ability to communicate. The information explosion is the most compelling reason to work on communications.

Total Talk Turn-Offs

It is hopeful to think that although you have met people who use these turnoffs, you have not done them yourself. These are examples of how *not* to communicate:

Unsolicited Advice; "Let me tell you what I would do."

Prophesies; "You will hate yourself tomorrow."

Hijackings; "You think you had a bad day? Wait while I tell you what happened to me today."

Reassuring Squelches; "A year from now you will look back and laugh."

Contradictions; "You aren't tired, you couldn't be."

Interrogations; "Why did you do that? Why didn't you talk to me first? What was going on in your head?"

Diagnosis; "You're only saying that because you're tired. You really don't mean it."

Sermons; "The money you are spending on clothes would clothe an orphanage."

Epilogue

The Faith-based Approach to Leadership

The spiritual approach to leadership is an adaptation of a diagram of the spiritual approach from the writings of George Barna.

It involves the physical, mental, emotional, and spiritual parts of a leader/manager's life.

These four parts of life involves seeking, establishing, advocating, harmony, recovery and method.

To write about this in any detail will have to be the subject of a new book. It is enough that the reader will think about the spiritual approach to leadership

A Final Note

You should plan what you want in your life. Whatever you plan for can happen. If you do not specifically plan for what you want you will go through your life just taking what will come. I know that you do some planning because you are reading this book.

To make your plan I recommend that you plan for three years at a time. Drop a year off at the end of the year and add a new year to your plan. If there were specific items that you did not achieve during the first year, add them back to your plan. You may have to add back specific items for a number of years.

At the age of 17, I made my first plan under the instructions of Ora Clark, one of my high school teachers. There was one item I put in my first plan that I did not achieve until I was age 28.

Make your plan very specific. If you want a BMW car, put it in your plan. Be specific as to what model and what color.

There may be some general items in your plan. Some of these may be labeled as your goals. Examples: Do you want a job where you can get to the top? Do you want a job where you work for yourself? Do you want to manage others? Do you want to travel?

Assess your abilities. Analyze your motivations. List your job specifications. The following is a life exercise, I urge you to use it.

Life Exercise

Directions: These eight sections represent the balance of your life. For each item, rank your level of satisfaction from 0 to 10.

0 1 2 3 4 5 6 7 8 9 10

____Physical Environment   ____Friends and Family

____Fun & Recreation   ____Health

____Personal Growth   ____Money

____Significant Other   ____Career

Remember:

Sometimes you are the Pigeon; Sometimes you are the Statue!

Appendix One

Ancient Writings to Assist Management

Decision
James 1:5, 6
Proverbs 3:5, 6

Fear
Hebrews 3:5, 6
Ephesians 6:10-18

Turmoil
Isaiah 26:3, 4
Philippians 4:6, 7

Weariness
Mathew 11: 28, 29
Psalm 23

Loneliness
Isaiah 41:10
Hebrews 13:5, 6

Sorrow
2 Corinthians 1:3-5
Romans 8:26-28

Suffering
2 Corinthians 12:8-10
Hebrews 12:3-13

The Golden Rule
Matthew 7:12

Relationships
Colossians 3:22-4:1

Professional Principles
Psalm 15
Proverbs 3:1-12

Danger
Psalm 91
Psalm 121

Christian Love
1 Corinthians 13

Responsibilities
Romans 12
Romans 13

Prayer
Matthew 6:5-15
Matthew 6:25-33

Generosity
Proverbs 11:24

Confrontation
Proverbs 28:23

Faith
Mark 9:23

Goals
Philippians 3:12-14

Loyalty
Proverbs 27:18

Rejection
Matthew 21:42

Wealth
1 Timothy 6:17-19

Temptation
1 Corinthians 10:13

Anxiety
Philippians 4:6,7

Leadership
Matthew 20:25-28

Appendix Two
Useful Books

Barna, George. (2001)*The Power of Team Leadership: Achieving Success Through Shared Responsibility.* New York: Random House Inc.

Barrs, Jerram. (1983) *Shepherds and Sheep: A Biblical View of Leading and Following.* Downers Grove: InterVarsity.

Blanchard, Kenneth and Norman Vincent Peale. (1988) *The Power of Ethical Management.* New York: William Morrow and Company.

Blenkinsopp, Joseph. (1995) *Sage, Priest, Prophet: Religious and Intellectual Leadership in Ancient Israel.* Louisville: Westminster John Knox.

Burke, H. Dale, (2004) *Less Is More Leadership: 8 Secrets to How to Lead & Still Have a Life,* Eugene, Oregon: Harvest House Publishers,

Charan, Ram. (2004) *Profitable Growth Is Everyone's Business : 10 Tools You Can Use Monday Morning.* New York: Crown Publishing Group.

Collins, Jim. (2001) *Good to Great: Why Some Companies Make the Leap... and Others Don't.* New York: Harper Collins.

Dinkmeyer, Don C. (1996) *Leadership by Encouragement.* Delray Beach: St. Lucie Press.

Dodd, Brian J. (2003) *Empowered Church Leadership: Ministry in the Spirit According to Paul*. Downers Grove: InterVarsity.

Eims, Leroy. (1996) *Be the Leader You Were Meant to Be*. Wheaton: Victor.

Fluker, Walter E., ed. (1998) *The Stones that the Builders Rejected: The Development of Ethical Leadership from the Black Church*. Trinity Press International.

Ford, Leighton. (1991) *Transforming Leadership: Jesus' Way of Creating Vision, ShapingValues and Empowering Change*. Downers Grove: InterVarsity.

George, Bill. (2003) *Authentic Leadership: Rediscovering the Secrets to Creating Lasting Value*. Valley Forge: Jossey-Bass.

Green, Hollis L. (2010) Sympathetic Leadership Cybernetics, Nashville:GlobalEdAdvance Press.

Green, Hollis L. (2010) Transformational Leadership in Education. Nashville: GlobalEdAdvance Press.

Greenleaf, Robert K. (1996) *On Becoming A Servant-Leader*. San Francisco: Jossey-Bass Publishers.

Gunderson, Gary, (2004*) Boundary Leaders: Leadership Skills for People of Faith*, Minneapolis: Fortress Press

Hastings, Wayne A. (2004) *Trust Me: Developing a Leadership Style People Will Follow*. New York: Random House Inc.

Hersey, Paul and Kenneth Blanchard. (1993) *Management of Organizational Behavior*. Englewood Cliffs, NJ: Prentice-Hall.

Hughes, R. Kent. (1987) *Living on the Cutting Edge: Joshua and the Challenge of Spiritual Leadership.* Westchester: Crossway.

Hybels, Bill. (2001) *Courageous Leadership.* Grand Rapids: Zondervan.

Kouzes, James and Barry Posner. (2003) *The Leadership Challenge for Christians.* Valley Forge: John Wiley and Sons.

Lewis, Phillip V.(1996) *Transformational Leadership.* Nashville: Broadman & Holman.

Malphurs, Aubrey. (2003) *Being Leaders: The Nature of Authentic Christian Leadership.* Grand Rapids: Baker.

Malphurs, Aubrey. (1996) *Values-driven Leadership: Discovering and Developing Your Core Values for Ministry.* Grand Rapids: Baker.

Marshall, Tom. (2003) *Understanding Leadership.* Grand Rapids: Baker.

Merritt, James. (2002) *How to Be a Winner and Influence Anybody: The Fruit of the Spirit as the Essence of Leadership.* Nashville: Broadman & Holman.

Meyer, Paul and Randy Slechta. (2002) *The Five Pillars of Leadership: How to Bridge the Leadership Gap.* Brentwood: FaithWorks.

Nelson, Alan.(2002) *Spirituality & Leadership: Harnessing the Wisdom, Guidance, and Power of the Soul.* Colorado Springs: Nav Press.

Sanders, J. Oswald. (1967) *Spiritual Leadership*. Chicago: Moody.

Senske, Kurt. (2003) *Executive Values: A Christian Approach to Organizational Leadership*.Minneapolis: Augsberg/Fortress.

Soder, Roger. (2001)*The Language of Leadership*. Valley Forge: John Wiley and Sons.

Toler, Stan and Jerry Brecheisen. (2002) *Lead to Succeed: New Testament Principles forVisionary Leadership*. Kansas City: Beacon Hill.

Towns, Elmer. (1992) *The 8 Laws of Leadership*. Lynchburg: Church Growth Institute.

Woods, C. Jeff. (2001) *Better Than success: 8 Principles of Faithful Leadership*. Valley Forge: Judson Press.

About the Author

Distinguished Professor, Theodore H. Kittell, PhD, JD, DLitt, PhD, PhD, taught graduate courses at Oxford Graduate School, Tennessee Wesleyan College and Bristol University. He has five earned doctorates, three master's degrees, and a bachelor degree. He also has certificates from Harvard Business School OPM, and AACC Counselor. Dr. Kittell was honored as a Scholar in the Oxford Society of Scholars.

Dr Kittell has been admitted to the Bar to practice law in Minnesota and California. He is an expert witness in healthcare management, has been a consultant for the Tennessee Board of Health for Nursing Homes, and was a licensed Nursing Home Administrator. He has served on various health related boards and commissions, and is affiliated with many professional associations. Throughout his business career he has been active in Kiwanis or Rotary Clubs and was recognized as a Paul Harris Rotary Fellow.

Dr. Kittell's experience includes 27 years as a hospital executive, two decades of experience as a lawyer, and ten years experience as a consultant in healthcare, education and management. His fascinating childhood growing up with the Navajos in New Mexico has added to his rich life experiences.

Dr. Kittell has written numerous papers in healthcare management, men's studies, assisted suicide and the right to die. Among his published books are: *Christianity and Management, Poems No. 1,* and *Philosophy and Philosophers.*

www.ingramcontent.com/pod-product-compliance
Lightning Source LLC
LaVergne TN
LVHW011425080426
835512LV00005B/274